Tea Leaves of the Soul

Dianne Kennedy
Tea Leaves of the Soul

Acknowledgements

My heartfelt thanks to Fay Forbes for her wisdom, encouragement and meticulous editing, and especially for her gently nudging me along the road to self-belief. Her undying love of literature continues to inspire members of the Devonport Writers' Workshop, to whom I also say thank you for your support and Tuesday nights' entertainment.

Thanks also to Dr Kristen Lang. Her workshops provided the catalyst for some of the poems and her advice was invaluable.

Some of these poems have appeared in different forms in anthologies produced by the Writers' Workshop, Devonport.

For Sean and Naiche

Tea Leaves of the Soul
ISBN 978 1 76041 110 7
Copyright © text Dianne Kennedy 2016
Cover: *Into the Light*, original painting by the author

First published 2016 by
Ginninderra Press
PO Box 3461 Port Adelaide 5015 Australia
www.ginninderrapress.com.au

Contents

Life Drumming… 7
  Life Drumming 9
  Workplace 10
  The Songstress 11
  The Bag Lady 13
  Love's Hands 14
  Silence 16
  The Warrior Walyer (Tarenorerer) 17
  The Dying Villa 19
  Two Lives in Quilt 20
  Rebuilding 22
  The Sentinel 24
  (Un)wells of Coal Seam Gas 25
  Elegy to the Black Cockatoo 27
  Death of a Queen 29
  A Woman of Substance 31

Raw Material… 33
  Raw Material 35
  Winter Reading 36
  My Grandmother: the Artist 37
  Memories of Grandparents 39
  The Toy Box 41
  Legacy 43
  Perceptions 45
  Lost Intimacy 46
  Final Storm 47
  The Call 48
  The Tramp 49
  For Jill 52

The Pendant	54
The Bowl	57
The Jigsaw Puzzle	59

The Way Back to Words… 63

The Way Back to Words	65
The Call of the Mountain	66
The Escape	68
The Final Touch	70
The Box Beneath the Bed	72
The Poet	74
If…	75
Haiku on Ageing	77
College Car Park 11 a.m.	78
If love…	79
Day Room Observations	80
Time:	84

Life Drumming…

Life Drumming

Drums that thrum on the nightclub floor
Take my spirit away to a distant shore
Where time does not turn to the tick of a clock
Where a house is not bound by bars or a lock
Where emotions expressed are not cause for shame
Where nature provides simple toys for a game
Where dancers stomp barefoot the rhythm of song
Where voices in harmony rejoice all night long
Where life is an entwining of legend and law
Where sufficient is enough, no craving for more
Where Mother Earth is the giver of all that folk need
Where prestige is in sharing, not in wealth or by greed
Where once for a while it was my fortune to be
Drumming softer back then on a rock by the sea.

Workplace

Mechanical cogs
Nuts and wheels
Chips and disks
Rods and reels
Each installed
To play its part
Churning production
At industry's heart
Pounding loyalty
Over the years
Turning and burning
Creating careers
Till time requires
Slight modification
Or replacement of
Old installation
No recycling
Tossed in a bin
No proffered regrets
Profits to win
Dole queues grow
Diminishing cash
Sacrificial workers
Corporative trash.

The Songstress

Tyrant love
Dictated
Remonstrated
Incarcerated
Bound her in barbed-wire chains
Of filial bondage.

At twenty-five she
Smashed the locks
Bent the bars
Launched herself to liberty.

Soaring adventurous skies
To foreign rebirth
She hovered; heeded a call –
He flung her down to earth.

Broken-winged she came
To bury his corpse
To bear the guilt
Of his brutal pledge.

Her shattered psyche
Now finds solace
In nightclub's gloom.
Sorrow of youth's loss
Slices listening hearts
Within the hazy room.

Her tortured dreams
Portrayed in purest note,
Her choking fingers
Crush the microphone throat,
As every evening
For over twenty years
Hatred cloaks harmonies,
Songs drown in tears.

Sire's sin continues to compel
The paying of her painful dues.
Doleful
Soulful
Jazz lady
Sings only the blues.

The Bag Lady

Woollen-coated Boadicea
slices city crowds
with her chariot –
        pushed, not ridden,

bearing rug-wrapped possessions
beneath plastic protection,
like her calm façade she
        keeps history hidden.

Statuesquely feminine,
forward thrusting
as if compelled by an
        unconscious call;

eyes focused ahead,
hair breezily flowing,
her ageing beauty commands
        respect by all.

It is not for battle
she is driven along,
nor vengeance seeking for a
        daughter's cruel plight;

she flees painful memories
in city-soiled streets;
a park bench or dark hallway
        hard comfort at night.

Love's Hands

(in memory of the SIEV-X victims: 19.10.2001)

Her hands softly cupped the downy head
as she cradled the newborn life.
His fingers stroked love, his eyes aglow
in wonderment at one with his wife.
The family, like a Christian Christmas scene,
depicted peace in an ideal world;
but outside the storm of war drew near
as fanatics' fatal flags unfurled.

Her hands held tight the child to her breast
to muffle the infantile plea.
His fingers hastened flight in the moonless night
as from home they were forced to flee.
Across lands and seas, they faced friends and foe,
guided only by hope's flickering lamp.
They finally found shelter in a foreign land
in an over-crowded refugee camp.

Her hands gripped constantly those of her child
to shield her from conditions there.
His fingers passed over the last cash they had
to secure safe passage to somewhere.
How could officials turn a blind eye then
as the over-crammed vessel set sail?
Did anyone warn the women and men
of the dangers this trip would entail?

Her hands clung desperately as the boat broke apart,
one to him, one grasping their daughter.
Frozen fingered he felt them slip silently away;
love drowned in the deep southern water.
The victims lost in murky depths that day
numbered three hundred and fifty-three;
their crime was paid flight from the horrors of war,
seeking a place where families grow free.

The hands of those who were found alive
now reach up for solace in prayer,
and finger-like poles of painted wood stand tall
reflecting the respect of people who care.
Asylum finally granted, he now walks alone
in a land which must share his pain
for the loss of tiny fingers which once clutched his
and soothing soft hands he'll not hold again.

Silence

Silent – why not?
Who here needs to share memories:
the tolling of the mission bell
summoning to lessons about white man's hell?

Silent – why not?
Who here needs to feel the batons' blows
in protests against barriers of colour and race,
the penalty paid: prison and disgrace?

Silent – why not?
Who here needs to listen and to heed
an old man's warnings of white man's greed;
of guns replacing a helping hand;
the laying waste of our beloved land;
of a Bible being justification for war;
of using sacred land as a toxic trash store;
of atomic tests with no tribal consultation;
of mines desecrating a once proud nation;
of proposals for establishing nuclear stations
with no regard for future generations;
of empty talks of reconciliation
which deny any rights of negotiation;
of custodial deaths from boots and noose –
I could shout it all, but what's the use?

Silence? There is none inside my head;
it pounds with the sounds of words unsaid.

In 1831, influenza took the life of a young Tasmanian Aboriginal woman on Swan Island. For a few years she had challenged the authority of *lutetawin* – the white man – who had killed or imprisoned most of her people. After escaping from sealers, she led a small band against the invaders, mostly in the Rubicon area. In truth, she was a patriot, a warrior, and a free spirit. The sealers called her Walyer; her name was Tarenorerer.* This poem is to honour her spirit.

The Warrior Walyer (Tarenorerer)

Tarenorerer, what song
do you sing?
Is it a dirge for a bird
with a shattered wing
whose fantasy of flying
southern free skies
plummets to earth under
lutetawin's lusting eyes?

Tarenorerer, do you
sing a love song?
Or were you taken too young
from where you belong,
exchanged to pale sealers for
dogs and flour,
ravaged and slave worked
every day, every hour?

Tarenorerer is now an
anthem your tune,
hummed as you huddle
beneath winter's cold moon
with patriots you lead
against insurgents too strong?
Your words when captured
reflect a rebel song.

Tarenorerer is there
sorrow on your breath
as you hover ever closer
to a pitiful death –
not by rifle nor spear,
no such warrior release:
they finally defeat you
with white man's disease.

* *The Aboriginal Tasmanians*, Lyndall Ryan, 2nd edition, 1996, Allen & Unwin

The Dying Villa

Flakes of former
grandeur drop
to mingle with
lead-light shards
bejewelling splintered
veranda boards;
denuded walls
and fractured posts
testimony to
fortune's fragility.
Doors stubbornly
cling haphazardly,
shutters hang aslant.
Unhinged remnants
clatter and rattle:
loosened proclamations
of past prestige.
Like an ageing actress
nattering and bragging
of ancient accolades,
she reclines and declines
on earthen bed,
her skeletal features
defiant in former dreams;
yet reality rips
her façade asunder
and emptiness abounds
beyond board bandaged eyes
as body and soul die and decay;
      even the ghosts have gone.

Two Lives in Quilt

I

Rising from her quilt of silk,
matching sheets and pillow case
she bathes to take away the trace
of tossing tormented sleep;
then drives from stately home to meet
companions for coffee and croissants
at her preferred prestigious restaurant;
loudly complains of last night's rain
pounding on the lead-light pane
disrupting rest, but far worse still
was that thing which made her feel quite ill:
a shattered stitch of silken thread
towards the base of her queen-sized bed
destroying dreams and the embroidered rose.
Of course like her company she knows
the working classes have no idea
how to handle quality and it is clear
her husband will tell the servant to go
for he is a forceful, resourceful CEO.
She'd forgiven foul language and frequent spilled milk
but never could she pardon that tarnished quilt.

II

Rising from her tawny quilt
and sheets of white and black
she stretches, arches her aching back
knowing she must seek a softer bed
and a warmer pillow for her head
now winter is on the way;
breakfast, courtesy of a classy café,
where last night she'd lifted a garbage lid and
removed the gourmet treat well hidden,
sufficient to relieve today's hunger pains;
she is pleased the evening's pelting rains
came from an appropriate direction
for her shelter to provide protection.
Carefully she folds the newspaper sheets
into bundled rolls, tidy and neat,
stashes them behind an old iron rack
and with a contented sigh turns back
to the treasure which yesterday she found
on a nearby stretch of vacant ground,
on four centre panels in smudged print: MILK;
gratefully she stows her cardboard quilt.

Rebuilding

Beth beat the boys at woodwork,
then fell in love with Jack.
At twenty-five with four children alive
they lived in a run-down shack.

Beth was aware she was useless
for daily he told her so;
made her understand with the back of his hand
then off to a bar he would go.

Bruised Beth would take a hammer,
some nails and a chunk of wood.
Hurt was drowned by the thumping sound;
the items she made were good.

Table and chairs were created,
four bunks and a huge double bed.
Jack said they were plain and added more pain,
sneering at the tears she shed.

Beth in desperation decided
to construct a simple thing.
After spicing Jack's meal no remorse did she feel
as she removed her wedding ring.

Beth placed it and Jack in the box
when the children were tucked in bed;
dragged it down a hill steep, she buried it deep.
'Your dad's gone,' next morning Beth said.

The shack now shines through the trees,
the children are happy and bright.
Rustic Wares reads the sign and business is fine
and Beth sleeps soundly at night.

The Sentinel

A tall stark sentinel stands proud,
guardian and protector to those who throng
from wind tossed seas to river's calm;
it flashes in time to the blackbirds' song.

As darkness descends the birdsong fades
and the beacon alone breaks the solace of night
while southward the city twinkles and glows
in a myriad of man-made starry lights.

When dawn slowly sweeps the cliffs to the east
the blackbirds trill to welcome the day.
Below the blue water is speckled by white
as gulls dive and swoop in squawking display.

The gulls' plaintive cries shatter the skies
and sad history seems to be sealed in their song
as they soar over cliffs and down to the shore
linking present to past and a people long gone.

The soft sands whisper the same mournful dirge
for the fate of the ones who called this place home
who were fed by the bounty of a clear crystal river
near tree dressed shores washed by unsullied foam.

Only memories now live in the native birds' song
and secreted in soil under lawns foreign grassed;
but forward in time the aged sentinel may stand:
a solitary remnant of other people now passed.

(Un)wells of Coal Seam Gas

Fiery tears flow from
faucets across the land
as Mother Earth weeps
and bleeds black blood.

Pylon needles pierce her flesh,
tearing the life force
from her tortured womb
to satisfy government greed.

Father Sun shrieks his offer
of intensifying rays;
wasted warmth shimmers
on man's pipe dreams of power.

Wind whines a desperate plea
to tame his own turbulence;
his proffered gift too falls
on dollar deaf ears.

Moon mourns the insanity,
gathers her tidal warriors.
Thunder and Lightning
lead the howling hordes.

Sun showers forests
with flaming arrows;
he scorches waterways
desert dry.

Earth's tears rain
raging torrents;
her heaving body
rips, gaping wide.

His heat shield stolen,
Sun hastens life's final throes;
yet arrogant man admits no guilt
in the tragedy of Earth's fatal woes.

Elegy to the Black Cockatoo

When forests die
and you are gone
my kind will walk alone.

No thrum of wings
will rent the sky;
no pine cones tossed
from branches high;
no shrieking song,
no contented sigh;
they will be alone.

Will they gaze to where
tall trees once stood;
tread barren earth
not on lush wild food?
Shall silence burn
their saddened minds
in a bare world wrecked
by being over-mined
as they walk alone?

But for now my
treasured totem one
we share sparse time
beneath scorching sun
and for a while
my spirits soar
while flora and fauna
still endure.
And yes, mankind
may somehow survive
yet I fear your kind
in dreams alone
will be alive.

Death of a Queen

She ruled her dominions over eons of change,
being born one of many up on the range;
her prowess and power apparent to all
as stately she stood in nature's green hall.
Her towering body reached high to the gods;
her feet firmly planted in mossy soft sods.
Her branches brushed tenderly those of her kin;
beasts and birds found sheltering haven therein.

Perhaps when the first ones beheld her might
they set her aside as a sacred site;
or was she a beacon to guide the way
if from forested tracks any one would stray?
Her gigantic girth would hold them in awe,
her lofty head hidden to those on the floor.
Her grandeur and beauty they would surely revere
with the respect of a people who hold nature dear.

Her land was then settled by the newly arrived;
some took up battle and fought by her side
demanding life rights for one so stately and old –
pleas for her kingdom dropped on ears, dollar cold.
Companions were slaughtered by enemy troops;
her domain was divided into distinct forest coups.
Her lonely life spared by caring people's desire
until her crashing defeat from a perilous fire.

An out of control burn-off raced up the slope,
gathering speed and widening its scope.
Desperate attempts were made, so they swear,
to save the grand lady swaying fearfully up there.
Her skirts licked by flames, her torso deep scarred;
her heart burst by heat, her skin brittle and charred.
The sovereignty of ages over once rich land around
finally shattered, she sank to a now barren ground.

A Woman of Substance

A woman of substance, the townsfolk said
of the lady who lived on the hill;
a well rounded dame with hyphenated name,
her late husband was a man called Will.

And late he was for she'd wed before,
he came in at number five.
There'd been Bob and Jack and Tom way back
before old Ben who'd been barely alive.

He passed away not long ere the day
when Will pledged his troth and his wealth.
In no time too his troubles grew –
he showed signs of diminishing health.

But the dame nursed him well and all could tell
she loved him deeper than most.
She said at his wake he'd be the last she would take;
she was a gracious and graceful host.

She shared her mansion with no other man
and rarely came down into town.
She died alone in her sumptuous home,
was buried in a gold satin gown.

Folk were hired to clear the estate;
what they found in the house and ground
made them determine the place must have vermin
so many pots of poison lay around.

Then they discovered under some covers
a book of deadly potions.
How could they suspect the lady held in respect?
They tried to dismiss the notion.

Still the law was called in and revealed her great sin;
raised bodies proved many a foul deed.
Recipes noting each name supported the claim:
she'd been a woman of much substance indeed.

Raw Material…

Raw Material

My mother's sculpting
was aided by habited ladies whose
white framed faces mocked age
                and earthly desires;

who preached devout fear
to potential novitiates of eternal virginity,
with the exception of one,
                a nun whose choices

were wrenched from her at fifteen
when parents, seeing sacrificial offspring
as promise of their own posthumous rewards,
                failed to fan out all fire.

Her insistence instilled doubts
in Mum's compliance to doctrines
of expectations for daughters;
                thus together they

pin-pricked the clay encasing my brain
allowing unsullied liquid to flow and ebb in
a tide of creativity and books
                and their own dispersed dreams.

Winter Reading

The book
        hard covered
        an encyclopaedia of reference
        a locked diary.

Questions elicited
        abrupt answers
        unsubstantiated by explanations
        unadorned by description.

Old binding
began to crumble;
ageing glue failed
to hold text firm.
Words tumbled forth
carried on dried
autumnal leaves.

Papery cheeks
softened by memory
as forbidden truths
splattered print
on to those blank pages
of our lives.

My Grandmother: the Artist

Her studio: the curtained end
of an upstairs hallway;
a calico seclusion permitting
family sounds to permeate.

A narrow window snared
brief daylight; a bare globe,
hanging low, insisted on constant
negotiations with shadows.

Pungent turpentine wafting
with the odour of wet oils
drew me often to observe
the meticulous mixing of colours
squeezed frugally from tubes
and mingled in minute portions
on the paint-encrusted palette.

Precision guided sabled strokes
as mind's picture was reproduced
on canvas in the clarity of the period:
clearly defined, carefully shaded
realism; no distortion of
design and no abstraction –
Grandma shunned such vagueness.

The space: a cramped, artistic domain
where racks of beginnings, progressions
and completions haphazardly
skirted the walls,
shelves buckled beneath books,
pencil shavings and paint splatters
escaped the confines
of the crumpled hessian mat.

Memories rest now in a rescued
worn silken smooth palette, and
fragments of nature encased in frames.

Memories of Grandparents

Straw hat ribboned beneath
chin to beat the breeze;
canvas chair and easel
set solidly in sand;
she sits, forward leaning, pencil
angled aloft in right hand;
trees which line the opposite shore
above rocks and fast flowing river
are sketched and blended
on anchored paper. A ship
rises on the horizon.
Standing, she observes,
absorbing the vessel's essence till it
overwhelms the estuary.
Her fingers swiftly
guide the image with precision:
the *Taroona* takes centre stage
on the page, its profile
sharp in contrast to the
hazy shapes beyond. It
berths upstream; she exhales,
gathers her hours into a
wicker basket, and smilingly
ambles towards the man who
patiently has passed the time
reclining beneath ancient pines
which define the beach's border.

Rousing, he leaves dreams
of seas sailed in his youth.
He stands, his hazel eyes
soften as he holds her smile.
Reverently he bends,
planting a discreet kiss
on her expectant cheek,
places her packages in the car,
holds the open door and her arm
as she lowers; seated, he
asks, 'Good?' Nodding, she
sighs contentedly,
her thoughts in prayerful
gratitude for the gift of art
and the soul who understands.

The Toy Box

The toy box of speckled wood
harboured hand-me-downs:
a tiny china tea set,
a baby doll called Doreen,
a kewpie too,
wool and reel for French knitting –
delicate feminine possessions
poured over with jealousy and delight
by friends.
Birthday additions included
a cooking set of minute pots and pans
and, as a guide for nurturing hands,
the intricacies of pastel pink
and yellow plastic
miniature appliances.

Doll numbers grew. Some became boys
with their own sets of toys.
Crudely sewn jeans replaced
the gown of walking-doll Carol
who, as a bride, had bleated *Mama*
when tilted. Had she been jilted
or was it in fear of her marital fate?
Soon aptly attired she sat astride
an outgrown bike repainted
and named Harley.

Pink-skinned blue-eyed Doreen
lost her head.
Kewpie touted tattoos.
The last porcelain arrival, exotic brown
Nina's raven curls were
transformed to dreadlocks;
she cast off her powder-blue dress
and stepped into leather.
Neen rode pillion to Carol, now Caz,
and on Harley they roared away.
The box became firmly locked
that day.

Legacy

It is right that your ashes were scattered
for what mattered in your life was the perception
of you by you. True, you
wore success like a suit of armour
to corporate battle – face masked,
frenetic task master blasting
deadlines at a frantic pace;
the race to win at all cost,
not caring for lost affection
by your rejection of tiny hearts
which smart and are scarred still.
Was it the blood which flowed and showed
more clearly within their small frames
that immersed you in fearful shame?

Dementia brought you down, bared the clown,
and the farce of your camouflaging acts,
by freeing the facts which had fuelled
the anger as you had duelled with truth,
and spurned all who held you dear
until fear drowned all filial devotion
in tears of lost childhood emotion.
In tremulous confusion you told
the cause of your shattered soul:
you were never whole.

Lies had fragmented your life
of distorted ideals. Your rambling
ancient voice revealed the overwhelming
self-consuming pride which for a lifetime
had been your guilt and your guide,
compelling you to deny the past:
the dark history you had held deep inside.

Perceptions

You rue the gloom of dark storm clouds;
I am drawn by magnetic hues
of velvet greys and glassy greens
and swirling blackish blues.

You rant against the rampant weeds;
the daisies revert my mind
to ringleted strands of childhood hair
in their linked embrace entwined.

You sense winter warmth from the fallen giant;
I weep for the slaughtered tree,
its noble limbs lying broken and torn
enshrouded in its wilting canopy.

Nature's night beacons beckon you not;
yet in their enchanting glow
I moon gaze to regain some serenity
and to escape my haunting woe.

As I see you caress a sleek machine
my brain is chain-bound like a slave,
lashed by stark memories of a metallic beast
plummeting youth to a premature grave.

Lost Intimacy

The desert drew you near to yourself
but like the stone shelf
shielding us from the sheer drop
to the purple and topaz scene below
the moment became blocked.
Your hand lost the clench of intimacy
between that place, and you and me.
It cooled, became limp in my grasp;
I had prayed for our love to last
like the sands below changing with time
to rock firm permanence.

Final Storm

The diminishing light
of encroaching summer rain
enshrouds our world
in a translucent shade of sallow,
fevered and pallid.
Or is image distorted
by love's death throes
casting garish shadows
over dreams turning to bile?
Your flushed face holds no smile;
no ripple of shared history
reflects in your eyes
as harsh sighs
punctuate the torrential tirade;
temples and brow
flood with pulsating blood;
the thunderous roar
of taunting vitriol
rips and shreds.
With lightning speed
your forked words
strike me to the floor.
All reason drowns
with the final sounds
of storming stamping feet
and the slamming of the door.

The Call

Like a child challenging the candle flame
my hand hovers in that indecisive moment
between being burned
or feeling heat as a mere hint of
fire's true force.

Repelling the ringing I turn away –
yet your number scorches my tormented mind
as through memory's tears
it flickers persistently on the phone.

The Tramp

In a rush through the rain
juvenile revulsion voiced my thoughts:
Erk, Mum, there's a tramp on our veranda!
Pausing, grasping his arm, I shushed,
pushed him and my disgust behind
while planning a course of attack.
With his tiny hand in mine, my son and I
stepped from the city street to our home.

S'all right, Mrs. I'll be gone when it stops.

The words, rasped from a face ravaged by
different storms, fuelled compassion.
I forced a smile, muttered through frozen lips,
That's okay, and shovelled my son inside
before his *But Mum!* dropped me deeper
into trenches of embarrassment.
Ashamed, I stood in the hall,
hanging our sodden coats on hooks.

My conscience leapt from
ledge to challenging ledge:
belief, charity, parental example.
What are you doing, Mum?
I carefully layered on the bread
ham, tomato and cheese;
took a paper cup and filled it
with hot sweet tea.

A *Yuk* was silenced by my matriarchal glare.
I took the fare and opened the door;
appeased my shame, accepted the blame
for youthful derision.
His trembling hands, encased in ragged mittens,
were as black as his buttonless coat;
a matching scarf failed to conceal
the frayed once-white shirt;

an ancient hat sat askew on rat-grey hair;
rough-cut tufts sprouted on his chin.
A paper-bag clad bottle tried unsuccessfully
to hide behind his tattered trouser legs;
scuffed shoes tapped to keep
unsocked feet warm.
You could come in, I began.
His eyes ran over the food in my hand.

*No love, I'm only here till the weather clears,
if that's all right.*

Of course, stay as long as you like, but if, I paused
reading something beyond pain in his eyes.
He grasped the food, nodded,
Bless you love, and your boy.
We parted, both moist-eyed at a most
basic moment of human joy.
Next morning only a paper cup and a plate
rested neatly in the corner.

The sun shone, I took my son's hand;
softly humming, I hoped that one day
he, too, may take a chance to understand.

For Jill

Feathers in perfect formation
lay on leafy soil;
plumage gleaming
blue, green and hues between;
golden dots defining
wing tip rims
of the vanished bird.
No bones, no flesh, no blood.
I gathered nature's strange gift.
As I cleaned and preened
the precious pinions
you drifted across my mind.

Disease stole your youth;
your body slowly shattered
in cruel decline.
Each downward step sparked
determination;
your spirit willed survival.
Your face still smiled.
Final distortion of movement
and words
denied your one
last pleasure:
your eyes now silently spoke.

In dreams I watched
feathers fall back
to forest floor
and enfold a dormant torso
lying there.
In a brief moment
it lifted, wings unfurled;
tranquil eyes held mine
till it turned and
with a screech triumphant
over deathly stillness
the reborn bird swirled
to light's circle
haloed beyond the trees.

Day dawned – you were gone.

The Pendant

You're a cat
for goodness sake!
I'm a dog person
whose shattered restraint
forced me to stray
to new beginnings.
Your chain was broken too.

I rediscovered you
when replacing drapes today;
had hung you there:
suspended memories,
knotting broken links over the rod –
over time I forgot.

You emerged – still screwed onto
your tiny timber trapezoid,
your fake gold untarnished
though more muted
than I remember;
your slanted hollow eyes
cheekily sinister;
your feline torso
elongated and sleek;
your fine whiskers
cutely curled skywards.

The last time you adorned me
you glittered against the black
of my arty-beat figure-hugging
sweater worn over matching
skimpy skirt, ebony stockings
and stylish stilettos.

You and my loose long hair
gilded that spot in the
half-light of the
emptying theatre:
we were younger then,
shinier.

I thought it was you who
attracted his stare
as his eyes lowered to there
during introductions.
His dark orbs smirked,
he flirted and seduced,
pierced my composure.

Confident in his own mystique
he held my hand – too long;
his strong fingers stroked, caressed.
His thumbs played circles on my palms
as his purred words ensnared.

Is that why I planted you up there:
a dangling signal to beware?
Or as an intimate memento
of a brief affair where
in final throes
no heart was broken;
slight sadness perhaps
but gratitude too at the reawakening
of primal emotions:
a reclamation of my former
passionate self.

So, what is to become of us:
relics and victims of
rushed unruly anticipation?
Your kitten comeliness
does beguile;
memories embedded in you
draw a smile

for they, like you,
are still a part of me –
and I know for certain
you will look great
against my new curtain.

The Bowl

Rim chipped,
its smooth interior
softly invites
the soothing caress of
circling fingers;
its outer shell
patterned in
pricked precision,
the tiny tan bowl
bears the colour and contours
of a speckled sparrow's nest
fitting snugly in hand.

A vagueness of
generations' passage
obscures its past;
hand-worked by
potter unknown.
Perhaps a first attempt,
or ceremonial,
or simply utensil,
its secret is secured
in the clay of its origin.

Modern memories lurk
of sugar or sauce
served with silver spoons,
small to avoid spillage;
of upturned play puddings
bound in Christmas ribbons;
of minute native dwellings
in pretend crockery villages;
of moulded mud houses
in sodden backyard;
of weaning kittens
whose rough-tongued lapping
daubed milk splatters
around its circumference –
cotton wool faces emerging
whisker dripping and satiated;
of cleaning and sorting
after death left a house
hollow, yet hallowed
in remembrance.

Bric-a-brac now in stacks for sale;
priceless possessions having
been bequeathed to kin.
Rescued, the tiny treasure
of a childhood blessed
now rests within my hand
and the cupboard of my heart.

The Jigsaw Puzzle

I am a jigsaw puzzle
nearly complete.

The securely slotted
straight edged border
bound me in tradition;
over time bits fell away,
some lost, some reinstated.

Background pieces
in russet desert shades
may prove difficult to place;
easier is the dappled green
of rain forest fern fronds
bordering burbling brooks.
Yet each landscape holds
the essence of me:
one – an awakening
amid sands as ancient as time;
the other filtering to tranquillity
the vibrant southern sun.

Meandering streams
rippling through
the patterned picture
nurtured:
the daughter, the mother, the lover.

There are rapids too –
one turbulently tumbling
into an abyss.

A pool shimmers amid
moss blanketed banks:
a soft landing leading
to new beginnings.

A cheeky bush orchid
peeks through
the woodland floor:
hope in a harsh domain.

A conifer clinging to a cliff
provides shelter
for a black cockatoo;
its head askew as if seeking
response to some screeched
philosophical notion.
I drank its native potion;
followed ancestral advice
and absconded to the hills,
escaping the sooty city
depicted midway
towards the base.

Steep outcrops overlooking
the pervading wilderness
contain caverns;
the darkness within
impenetrable protection –
these hold parts of me
which are mine alone.

On the lowest rows
trees become sparse, ragged,
as if swept by a windstorm;
yet within the surrounding
browning grass
flashes of minute flora
depict the determination
and fragility of life.
Mists begin to
obscure pictures,
pieces here are blank,
in the border gaps grow…
this must remain so
for that inevitable time
when my spirit
will need to fly free.

The Way Back to Words…

The Way Back to Words

Clay creations
        captured imagination;
words coiled,
        wound around pots:
poetry became fired
        in the kiln of my mind.

The Call of the Mountain

Like a magnet set in southern skies
        you drew me to you;
        your ancient face gazing westwards
        above hands poised in prayerful pose:
        a rock-firm link to ancestral times
        beckoning my nomadic soul.

    Calling; calling.

Occasionally I visited:
        walked your lower glades;
        sought solace in your shadows;
        climbed to your summit;
        passed hours marvelling
        at your lofty permanence –
        yet I did not stay.

Your pull persisted
        on yellow-dipped pinions
        of the black cockatoo;
        on the scarlet breast
        of the warbling winter robin;
        on the metallic plumage
        of the minute blue wren;
        and clearer still in the screeches
        of circling soaring eagles.

    Calling; calling.

Finally I succumbed:
        cast aside city bonds
        to nestle in the soothing
        shelter of your embrace.
        Words replaced worries,
        freedom dispelled fear.

You called,
        I came…
                I am home.

The Escape

An empty page
niggles on the desk;
a pen lies idle
nestled at its side;
while boots tramp
the welcoming track.

A screen glares
stark and blank;
the mouse reposes
on its mat;
while a jacket flaps
in freedom's breeze.

Confusion fades
as an eagle soars
above first footfalls.
Thoughts are washed
by warbles trickling
through branches.
Songs slice stillness,
enfolding and caressing
the senses.
While from on high
screeches cascade
drops of wonder
over my heart.

Feet skip, arms lift,
as cares drizzle
and descend
to become interred
under leafy earth.

A smile stretches lips
to half-moon;
clouds clear
from the soul;
eyes re-open
to pools of dreams.

Sorrow's stitches
slowly unravel,
replaced by gentle memories
embroidered in birdsong.

A fire is rekindled;
the spirit renourished.

Page and pen beckon;
screen and mouse wait.
At peace now
I come home to create.

The Final Touch

'Stop!' I moaned. 'This will never do.'
'But I am complete, you said it's true.'
Tears trickled from her puzzled eyes;
my irritation was not disguised.

She slinked softly yet surely into my precious space
Her hand seductively fingered my expectant face.

'You are a beauty,' I reassured.
'You do like my hair?' she demurred.
'Yes,' I nodded, 'though it's overstated.'
'Oh you would say that,' she berated.

Her long golden tresses temptingly begged for my touch
I twirled a curl round my trembling hand, I loved her so much.

I yanked out that adjectival lock;
she landed a slap, we were both in shock.
'Sorry,' I said, 'it made you look like a whore.'
'Well,' she pouted, 'it's one you won't score.'

As she pounded angrily towards the huge cheval glass
I noted quite sadly her oversized adverbised arse.

'Ow!' she howled when I pointed it out.
I flicked them off while ignoring her shout.
She smiled when upon a further inspection
she viewed a trim and taut reflection.

Like a lion I then attacked some loose similes;
like a beggar she pleaded on bended knees.

To metaphors some of these were transposed
some were retained, the remaining disposed.
'Happy now,' she sneered, 'that I feel dull and plain?'
'Yes, I think so,' I smirked. 'I feel content and sane.'

I pressed *save* on the keyboard,
took the draft from the printer;
held a pen aloft,
I heard her whimper:
'Don't touch me again,
you perfectionist fop,
for the one thing you don't know
is just when to stop.'

The Box Beneath the Bed

What if all those pieces of paper
containing snippets of random thoughts
became partnered in perfect formation
to portray verses of varying sorts?

Some might join into stanzas
of similar lines once composed
to reveal ideas deeply profound
and become cleverly transposed

to sonnets extolling some virtues
so well expressed they challenge the Bard,
or to odes in praise of things mundane –
surely that could not be too hard.

A limerick or two might emerge;
maybe one Aussie bush ballad or more
for the box from beneath my bed is bulging
with scraps escaping on to the floor.

What if an epic lurks therein
just waiting for release?
Or little leftovers form haiku
and bring my poor mind some peace

from the guilt of withholding wisdom
ensconced in succinct scribbled words;
for such literary wealth to be wasted
must be considered truly absurd.

What if I give the box a good shake,
stir its contents round and round,
would works of genius burst forth
and would I gain great literary renown?

What if among those scraggy pieces
lies that one thought which needs to be said?
It's starting to sound like too much hard work…
I'll just push it back under the bed.

The Poet

Sounds pour over me
soothing
refreshing
like a forest waterfall
splashing
enmeshing
body and soul
in a gentle hold.

The beauty and truth
of reality shimmers in
the sparkling droplets
of your words.

Dewdrops descend
awakening petals
as they pass.

Blossoms unfold
easing themselves
to enlightenment.

If…

If I hadn't accepted the ticket
my best friend gave to me
she would have been the lucky one
and my conscience would still be free.

If I hadn't won that holiday:
three nights at the remote retreat
to languish in splendour and luxury
my reputation might still be complete.

If I had not passed the hours idly,
nor partaken of several huge meals,
then slowly filled the open-air spa
at that spot nestled in lonely hills,

I might not have snoozed in the suds
stirring only to sip some more wine,
while feeling the thrill of a hundred wee jets
soothing that age-bloated body of mine

to the point where I rose like a nymph
from the murky depths of my brain
and danced naked around in circles,
body and soul releasing all pain.

Thus I sang and danced round and round,
in rapture I twirled on those tiles
till that awful inkling I was not alone –
opened eyes met with seven broad smiles.

Too late to hide ample frame –
I must have looked like a balding baboon;
for it was not just my space now exposed
to adventurers in the hot air balloon.

My life flashed before me that day
as did plenty of my parts to the throng;
if only I had been in my aged-twenty skin
they might have thought me entrancing and strong;

all they saw was my mad mature dash
and a spectacular dive into the brine
as the suds and I became redder and redder –
not only from the spilled bottle of wine.

Haiku on Ageing

Wrinkles not pimples
dimple facial covering:
valleys of wisdom.

Soul's curtained windows
deny communication:
frustration within.

Youth's falsities gone:
long lashes, full lips, fake nails
displaced by dentures.

Foetal dementia
curls stiffened muscles and bones
back to beginnings.

College Car Park 11 a.m.

Shuffling feet trailing aged stiffened paws through youth's domain;
a seventh limb steadying the trail of their daily jaunt.
Rubber history sniffed through cracked nostrils:
allowance for faithful togetherness united tenderly by soft leash.
No designated leader:
        devotion binds the two.

The one:
wind defying hat adhered to head bent,
warmly clad shoulders stooped against gusts;
steps on paved memories of swampland;
whispers affection to his sole companion
on this break in their slow
        journey to life's exit.

The other:
eyes curtained by cataracts feels comfort,
cherishes the love rippling his restraint;
resists the urge of reversion to youthful play;
round torso rolling and swaying, slack leashed stays
beside his master's stronger limb to
        help balance the way.

Though each day bears inevitability on its back
and the yoke of ageing years is by both hard borne,
their peaceful hour strolled is a stark contrast
to the parked tense trappings of youthful scorn.
This pair share the vehicle of precious time,
        treasured though well worn.

If love…

If love be a raucous youth
rushing, gushing, crushing, flying –
trip it!

If love be a maudlin girl
dreaming, scheming, beaming, crying –
flip it!

If love be a business man
earning, yearning, spurning, lying –
kick it!

If love be a mature woman
boring, yawning, fawning, buying –
flick it!

But if love be ageing, female or male,
join in its journey for on calm seas they sail;
for ripe love is the sweetest, a most unique kind,
housed in deep knowledge within wisdom's mind.
No sinister purpose, it is honest and rare.
Look beyond ancient eyes and linger long there.
Then grasp it and clasp it and treasure it with care
lest life's flame flickers too soon and no love's left to share.

Day Room Observations

I

Doris dreams of dance halls,
country churches and charity do's;
her fingers drum out memories,
remembered rhythms tapped by her shoes.

Music had diminished isolation,
brought acceptance and even renown
when she had married her man and his land
and the neighbouring small country town.

Her talent graced many occasions:
christenings, the district debutante ball,
weddings, anniversaries and funerals –
Doris had accompanied them all.

Now Doris's keyboard is confined to her mind,
her table top transformed to treble and bass;
by joint stiffened digits thoughts' tunes are defined,
imagined pedals are tapped at the appropriate pace.
With eyes glazed in dreams, a serene smile on her face
Doris drifts back to another time and place.

II

Lightly nodding
        in sweet fragrance
tall, fragile,
nestling gently
        in the garden corner
blooms lily-like Linda
leaning slightly
        as if the tiniest breeze
might break her reedy stem;
she softly shares
        her wisdom and her strength.

III

Gentle velvety Verity
whispers only occasional words.
She sleeps and smiles,
obliges and obeys
        …but not every day.

Verity can be naughty
in sweetly devious ways:
sometimes sassy sayings
slip surprisingly from her lips
        …and blow everyone away.

IV

Day one:

        She said her name was Flo and she was
        only here for a day or so;
        her son and his wife would come
            on Sunday to take her home.

Day five:

        She loved a lively chat, spoke often
        of her house and loved cat;
        she looked forward to seeing them again
            on Sunday when she went home.

Day six:

        She sat all day there, watched, waited,
        nestled comfortably in her chair.
        Visitors came and went for it
            was Sunday, yet she was alone.

Day nine:

        Scones at morning tea were served;
        she said they had been her specialty.
        'If I could, I'd bake some for Sue and John
            for Sunday when they take me home.'

Day thirteen:

    Her family came today, for an hour,
    they didn't have much to say;
    they shrugged off queries about the cat;
        it was Sunday and still she stayed.

Day seventeen:

    Uttering not the usual complaint, she accepted
    the fitting of a safety restraint.
    'I miss my little cat,' she said,
        'but on Sunday I'll see her again.'

Day Twenty:

    Nurse asked about the cat, John mumbled
    that the vet had seen to that;
    then smiled at Sue, 'We can't stay long
        for Sunday is our busy day.'

Day twenty-four:

    Scones again, she did not eat, just sat and
    stared down at her feet.
    Tears spilled as she murmured how
        on Sunday she'd love to go home.

Day twenty-seven:

    The day room was bright, Flo did not show
    having passed on peacefully in the night.
    A grey car was sent to fetch her for it
        was Sunday, and Flo went home.

Time:

that indefinable distance of being
measuring life with pendulums pounding my mind
or cotton wool caresses soothing my psyche;
gauging the space from 'once was' to 'soon will be'
and beyond – cracking infinity's walls
as it comes cloaked in creeds
of incarnations, eternal rewards, or naught.
Time's end will be the ungrasped revelation.

www.ingramcontent.com/pod-product-compliance
Lightning Source LLC
Chambersburg PA
CBHW062145100526
44589CB00014B/1691